G.E.T. W.E.L.L.
S.O.O.N.

Space for Personalized Message

Get Well Soon: A Poem of Comfort

ACRONYM POETRY GIFT SERIES

By Macarena Luz Bianchi

Designed by María Paula Gabela

To receive a free ebook, exclusive content, more wonder, wellness, and wisdom, sign up for her *Lighthearted Living* e-newsletter at MacarenaLuzB.com and check out her other poems of self-expression, books, and projects.

ISBN: Hardcover: 978-1-954489-58-5 | Paperback: 978-1-954489-64-6

Imprint

Spark Social, Inc. Miami, FL, USA, SparkSocialPress.com

Ordering Information: Licensing, custom books, and special discounts are available on quantity purchases. For details, contact the publisher at info@sparksocialpress.com.

G.E.T. W.E.L.L. S.O.O.N.

A Poem of Comfort

ACRONYM POETRY GIFT SERIES

Macarena Luz Bianchi

Imprint
Spark Social Press

HOME MADE CANDLE

FOR HYGGE EVENING

My Dear Reader,

Not feeling well can be inconvenient and no fun.
So please remember you are cared for and loved,
through it all.

Enjoy,
Macarena Luz Bianchi

acrostic & acronym

ăk′rə-nĭm″ & ə-krô′stĭk

noun

A word formed by combining the initial letters of other words

poetry & poem

pō′ĭ-trē & pō′əm

nouns

A written set of words that convey ideas and emotions with vivid imagery and/or rhythmic sound

Definitions

comfort

com•fort | 'kəmfərt

noun

A state of ease and freedom from pain, constraint, or discomfort

hygge

hyg•ge | 'ho͞ogə, 'ho͝ogə

noun

A quality of coziness and comfortableness, giving rise to feelings of
contentment and well-being (from Danish culture)

Get well soon...
with extra kindness and patience!

Embrace this moment,
knowing you are cared for,
completely.

Take your time
to meditate and reflect.

Well wishes while you
heal and recuperate.

Emerge enhanced and encouraged
after slowing down and pausing.

Journal

Laughter may or may not be the best medicine but is worth playing with, thoroughly.

Loving comfort and healing vibes
are sent to uplift you along the way.

So please rest and recover
gently and quickly with...

Openhearted support and appreciation
for your healing journey.

Openminded opportunities
to learn and grow gracefully.

Now rest, be well, and get better soon
while taking extra good care!

G.E.T. W.E.L.L. S.O.O.N.
A POEM OF COMFORT

Get well soon... with extra kindness and patience!

Embrace this moment, knowing you are cared for, completely.

Take your time to meditate and reflect.

Well wishes while you heal and recuperate.

Emerge enhanced and encouraged after slowing down and pausing.

Laughter may or may not be the best medicine but is worth playing with, thoroughly.

Loving comfort and healing vibes are sent to uplift you along the way.

So please rest and recover gently and quickly with:

Openhearted support and appreciation for your healing journey.

Openminded opportunities to learn and grow gracefully.

Now rest, be well, and get better soon while taking extra good care!

❦❧

Thank you, Dear Reader!

Get Inspired & Stay Connected

To receive a free ebook, exclusive content, more wonder, wellness, and wisdom, sign up for her Lighthearted Living e-newsletter at MacarenaLuzB.com and check out her other poems of self-expression, books, and projects. ✨

Your Feedback is Appreciated

If you like this book, please review it to help others discover it. If you have any other feedback, please let us know at info@sparksocialpress.com or via the contact page at MacarenaLuzB.com. We would love to hear from you and know which topics you want in the next books. 🌻

About the Author

Macarena Luz Bianchi has a lighthearted and empowering approach and is affectionally considered a Fairy Godmother by her readers. Beyond her collection of gift books and poems, she writes screenplays, fiction, and non-fiction for adults and children.
She loves tea, flowers, and travel.

Subscribe to her Lighthearted Living newsletter for a free ebook and exclusive content at MacarenaLuzB.com and follow her on social media. 💕

Macarena Luz Bianchi

Gift Book Series

ACRONYM POETRY COLLECTION

- *Be My Valentine: A Poem of Love*
- *Congratulations: A Poem of Triumph*
- *Friendship: A Poem of Appreciation*
- *Get Well Soon: A Poem of Comfort*
- *Happy Birthday: A Poem of Celebration*
- *Intimacy: A Poem of Adoration*
- *Sympathy: A Poem of Solace*

POETRY COLLECTION

- *Dear Dad: A Poem of Appreciation*
- *Glorious Mom: A Poem of Appreciation*
- *Gratitude Is: A Poem of Empowerment*
- *Gratitude Is: Poem & Coloring Book*
- *The Grateful Giraffes: What is Gratitude?*

Also available for children and in Spanish:
Colección de Poesía I.